S0-BOM-881

THE ROOMS WE MAKE OUR OWN

THE ROOMS WE MAKE OUR OWN

TONI MIROSEVICH

Firebrand
Books
Ithaca, New York

Earlier versions of several of these poems and stories have been published in the follow-ing literary magazines: *Alchemy, Ink, Kenyon Review, Magazine, SFSU Review, Santa Clara Review, Seattle Review, Transfer,* and *ZYZZYVA;* and in the chapbook *Trio: Toni Mirosevich, Charlotte Muse, Edward Smallfield* (Specter Press).

Copyright © 1996 by Toni Mirosevich
All rights reserved.

This book may not be reproduced in whole or in part, except in the case of reviews, without permission from Firebrand Books, 141 The Commons, Ithaca, New York 14850.

Book design by Nightwood
Cover design by Lee Tackett and Debra Engstrom

Printed on acid-free paper in the United States by McNaughton & Gunn

10 9 8 7 6 5 4 3 2 1

Library of Congress Cataloging-in-Publication Data

Mirosevich, Toni.
    The rooms we make our own / Toni Mirosevich.
        p.   cm.
    ISBN 1-56341-080-X (paper : alk. paper). —ISBN 1-56341-081-8 (cloth : alk. paper)
        1. Working class women—Literary collections. 2. Lesbians—Literary collections.
PS3563.I716R66   1996
818'.5409—dc20   96-34564
                                                                        CIP

ACKNOWLEDGMENTS

Gratitude beyond measure to:

Frances Mayes, who provided literary life support for this work from start to finish; and to Michelle Carter, Marny Hall, Elly Bulkin, Nancy K. Bereano, Meredith Duke, Susan Synarski, Angrove Samsell, Ann Warren, and especially to Shotsy Faust—without her love and humor, life would be so much less.

for Shotsy

CONTENTS

ONE

TWO

THREE

FOUR

I think of my poems as my kiddo...

Stevie Smith, *Novel on Yellow Paper*

ONE

GANDHI JOINS THE WORK FORCE

With hose in hand, finger on the trigger, I rap
the head of the nozzle on the park restroom door,
yell, "Clean up," in the most masculine voice
I can muster, remove the tremor, notice small
nicks in the wood where the metal handle leaves
its mark.

After a moment they come out, one after another,
three men together who look up, instead of the
vice squad see a small woman with a pressure
washer and big boots trying to look tough. I
smile, offer apologies, God, I'm sorry, I just
have a job to do.

I fashion myself Gandhi, no work too demeaning,
no work beneath me, sold on the idea that by
cleaning johns I'm doing a service to mankind,
and well, mankind this certainly is, them on
their gay march to the sea, noses held high and
hang British rule.

Inside I blast away any vestige of romance, swab
toilets, do things my mother never intended me
to do, notice things are cleaner here than on
the women's side where the sticky condom lay on
the toilet seat next to the torn picture from
Playboy, you have got to be kidding. This is
where some guy got off?

It's not the group of three I fear, but the ones
like the guy at the last stop, who hears the
warning but doesn't make a sound, who stands in
mock surprise, his pants down at his ankles when
I come round the bend. "Without even the decency
to cover," my mother would say.

I picture Richard Speck, then Bundy, his good
looks, his boyish charm, and perfectly healthy
arm hung in a sling, asking young women, "Ma'am,
can you help me with my boat?" Forgetting about
Gandhi for a moment, I point my weapon, pray I
have enough water pressure to blow him away with
the rest of the dirt. (Are women more powerful
when they have equipment?)

Here, at this last stop, someone knocks on the
door. Remembering I'm preparing a love room,
I drop a couple extra deodorizing disks in the
urinal, do not reach for the pennies, decide to
leave the phone numbers up another day, what the
hell, small victories of intimacy. What did
Gandhi say? *Everything is possible with the power
of love.*

Madonna Joins The Work Force

What is it about a woman driving a truck?
(Haven't we always known how to maneuver?)

I jump down from the cab—do not discreetly place
my leg on the step, not some starlet here stepping
out of a limo ankle first, for gawkers to get a good look
at the gams—no I jump down, with what authority I
can muster. Other truckers, circled around the pumps,
see a small woman getting out of the *driver's* side
and it registers

their mouths so open birds could build.

I go about my business, every movement scrutinized,
like Madonna amid trucker paparazzi, stand with
my feet apart, expressionless (give them no entry)
shove the gas nozzle into the tank, resist the urge
to spit.

A guy pulls alongside, his rig parallels mine, his
face doughy, black stubbled, as if the toast were
left in too long, read on the side of his truck
that he works for Wonder Bread. (You are what you
transport.)

He shouts over at me, "Need some help with that
nozzle little lady?" Does this before he notices
that with thirty-five feet of trailer behind me

mine is longer than his.

I top off the tank, hop back into the cab, tuck
the gas receipt in the bodice of my black bustier.
Tooling out of there, I fail to nick the corners of
the building, fail to sideswipe the other trucks,
pull into traffic as smoothly as a mallard into
formation,

with all that remembered delicacy.

BETTY CROCKER JOINS THE WORK FORCE

They leave me in charge of the soup with the trust
of people who feed the hungry, who do this type of
work. I protest, ask for a lesser dish, but they
wave me off (as if it's an easy task to warm leftover split pea on an industrial stove, larger than
the toy model in pink plastic, the last stove I
touched).

On the door of the dining room a sign says, *This
is a soup line for women and children only.* The men
go elsewhere where they line up like men do at ball
games or job sites, without a woman's presence to
change their posture to predatory. Here the women
are safe. (Except for me and my pedal-to-the-metal
approach to cooking. What can you do to soup?)

Given the license to doctor, I open jars of spices,
like so many grass clippings, and put a little of each
in the large kettle, knowing I'll hit something, like
the trial dinners concocted on the toy stove, husband-
pleasers, made with every ingredient in the kitchen,
forced on the neighborhood's willing pets.

While the soup simmers I place plastic flowers on each
table, Betty always stressed presentation, arrange a
garnish dish, the sorry-looking radishes—raided from
some dumpster—which I've tried to fashion into rosettes
with a dull paring knife.

At six I go over to the door and greet them like a
hostess, like they've all been invited, pump each hand.
Most don't meet my eye, the obvious question there, a
strip search for clues, how did this happen to you? (As
if I deserve an answer, as if they deserve this soup.)

I ladle it up, my best effort, their only meal, realize
there's a problem when the bowls come back half full,
barely touched, with a sip notice the burnt taste in
each and every pea, and this now, what I've always
pictured: the husband unhappy, his accusatory look,
and no one but Betty to blame.

HERMES JOINS THE WORK FORCE

We stand around, a Blood Bank night crew with time
on our hands, not a lot of chatter, a little joke
here, a comment there, how the shelves look, if
the inventory's up, the latest baseball scores,
take your bets, hey, what about those Siamese
twins at UC, an operation that's taking gallons.

A call comes in, another stab wound at the General.
I grab six units off the shelves, pack them in ice,
like Hermes, god of thieves, steal from one group
to give to the next. And here we are, blood the
common denominator whether people like it or not.

Every job gets mundane, even this, rushing *O pos*
to the knife wound, the heart, people reduced to
the area of conflict on their bodies, and now it's
up to me, to mop up like a mediator, race to the
hot spots, patch up the wounds of the world.

I know the shortest route, time traffic lights,
careen into the hospital lot, wheel in the box of
blood, the double doors of the emergency exit like
a Western saloon, no time, no time, knock into
a man carrying some condolence gift who hesitates
before he picks up his package.

Hermes, the messenger, guided souls on their way
to Hades, the one god with an open-door policy, who
could come and go. I swing by the man, down into

the bowels of this particular hell, watch as people
step back from a box marked HUMAN BLOOD, this in
the age of AIDS, when even a box gets stigmatized.

Once I get past the ER desk, the pathway's clear
all the way to the lab where I give them the cold *AB
neg*, the backup *O pos*, each unit logged in, tagged
and soon poured into the new body where it gets
reheated, warmed up again. The lab tech smiles,
says, "When it rains it pours," and we laugh at the
weak joke, our only way to leaven.

As I leave another ambulance pulls in. I forget
to say a prayer, hope the siren isn't sounding for
someone I love, but why should it matter? I make
a mental note to call the hospital later, to find
out how the knife wound did, and then, like Hermes,
I settle in for the return trip, bent on finding
a different route home.

FRIDAY JOINS THE WORK FORCE

We make our way through underbrush, me and the
head of tree operations, Golden Gate Park a lush,
green island we've washed ashore on. I tell him I've
done this kind of work before, been a treetopper in
the Northwest, though this is a lie, the only way women
get in. He looks at me, takes in my small frame,
slim wrists, neatly pressed carpenter's pants, well,
damn if I'm not going to look good in my rise to the top.

He picks the largest tree he can find, a redwood,
a skyscraper. I hear a small crack, splintering, like
a country yokel in the big city tilt my head up.
Above us, damage. The bough to be sawed off sways
in the breeze. I hum "Rock-a-bye Baby" to keep my
cool, notice he makes a little mark on his scorecard.

In my women in the trades support group, they say
imagine yourself triumphing, mind over matter, so
I see myself as Friday scampering up the palm, swift,
agile, my bare feet grooved into the bark. I grab
the bough like a brass ring, a gift for Crusoe though
I feel the sting, this subservience. Robinson has
all the power to decide.

He hands me the gear. I strap things on: cleats and
shimmying belt, rope, a chainsaw to hook on the side,

all trappings with which to make my ascent. He studies
me again. Yes, as far as strap-ons go, I'm missing
something key. I put my boot to the bark, wishing I
could climb out of this drama, out of this life, and
sit up there in an aerie, watch Robinson fend for
himself.

The wind comes up, no tropical breeze. I don't recall
how the story ends. Did they get past their differences,
were they saved? Did cannibals and crisis draw them
together? I give him my best smile, one that claims,
We're in this together, bub. "Alley-oop," he says, then
cups his hands together, gives me a leg up.

OPHELIA JOINS THE WORK FORCE

At 4:00 A.M. the pool house is damp, cavernous. All the
swimmers are still at home asleep, sheets wrapped
around their triangular chests, dreams of failure
or triumph. Their legs and arms jerk like puppies',
synchronized, each young man of the same mold: blond,
blue-eyed, and tortured.

Littering the locker room floor: tossed swimtrunks,
goggles, codpieces, remnants of the chase. As I sweep
up I hear a noise, catch a figure on the periphery,
my boss dropping by to check on the job. He wends
his way around the grounds, as thorough as Polonius
and as nosey, with his eye to the keyhole gets all
the evidence he needs.

Each day I watch the swimmers, their bodies switch-
blades sprung loose. They trip over my hoses, give
me dirty looks (as if it takes no grace to wield a
chlorine tank, come up with the right mix). I know
I don't belong, never the attitude of champions, all
that hope and shine—though somehow I'm sure I deserve
better than this.

In the half-light I ready the pool, hose down the
sides, arrange the floats, check the temp so they
will not chill. The leaves on the pool's surface
form a pattern, invite. I feel the pull, some place
free of concern—tired of Hamlet's histrionics,

always the serious look, always the furrowed brow,
never, *Hey, let's order out for pizza.*

I take off the gear, overalls, thigh-high
boots, the floral crown, without a stitch dive
into the deep end. Numbers pass by, no person left
to please, not Laertes, not the King, free of all
these men's demands.

The world below is easy, blue. I travel south, away
from Denmark, head toward the softer Mediterranean
climes. I swim toward the far shore, into the light,
where forms appear, angular, inverse pyramids capped
by halos of golden light.

They stare down with red rimmed eyes—sullen,
accusatory—as I come up for air.

VIRGINIA WOOLF JOINS THE WORK FORCE

With new Redwing boots, stiff overalls, cowhide
tool belt holding every drill known to man, every
hammer, hacksaw, wrench packed in, a struggle to
keep our waists above our knees, we knock on the
door of the weathered house, happy, full of purpose,
three women dressed in tools.

Inside we negotiate the crawl space, dance with knob
and tube, blow in gales of insulation, add a couple
of extra inches, pack her in tight, protecting the
old woman downstairs from the elements. "The sudden
bruise of the rain storm." V. Woolf.

Downstairs we weatherstrip each door, wrap the
water heater in a white fiberglass blanket like a
new babe in swaddling clothes, the loving touch,
the bare light in the garage a star in the east and
we, the three Magi, stop a moment to admire our
work. Could this be what Virginia meant by
"moments of being"?

Outside we hoist storm windows, double-paned, as
tight as Tupperware or as Saran Wrap on a bowl of
leftover beans, you couldn't get a better fit, her
house now a Volkswagen that would float on water.

from *The Waves* by Virginia Woolf

As our last duty we cut holes in the roof to put in
vents, forget which way the wind does blow. (Is that
in the manual?) We realize four days later they're
put in backward, so that rain coming down the
slant collects in the new "drains" on her roof.

With no leak untended, no draft or breeze, her
house as mild as a mall, the ceiling comes tumbling
down, and she, wrapped now in a soft pink blanket,
is insulated once and for all against the storm
inside and out, against the waves, the waves, the
waves.

So here we are and I offend someone right off the bat.

I'm at my friends' place in the Northwest, sharing in their open house on Christmas Eve. A group of us are gathered around the eggnog when another car pulls into the drive. Two women get out. Someone mentions one of the women has worked on the railroads for twenty-two years. No, that's not quite right. That's worked *for* the railroads, and in that preposition is the biggest difference. I hear *on* and think she's an *on*-the-railroads worker, which might mean she's a brakeman, which might mean the sound of steel on steel and those cute overalls, which might mean time spent in the caboose and swinging a red lantern and putting up with the boys.

The railroad woman comes in, plants herself in the doorway, has a stance that hasn't quite vanished with the punch of the clock. She calls out names in a booming voice, a voice she would have to have if she was an on-the-railroads person, yelling to others in the yard above the din of the tracks. She makes her way over through the knots of dykes to a group of us gathered around the eggnog bowl.

I say, loudly, too loudly, being a bit nervous, "So you work on the railroads."

The conversation stops, a great space opens, no one is on the track, the rails as deserted as they will continue to become as we move into the twenty-first century. There is no distant horn, no flashing light, no crossbar lowered; or it's as if a silent crossbar lowers, right in front of the car beams, stopping any forward motion and we both have to wait for the train to pass. But there is no train.

"Yes. I'm the one who works for the railroad." But her look says a lot more, like she thinks I'm making fun of her.

"No, really. I'm interested. My father was a fisherman. I was a truckdriver." As if this matters, as if this will connect us, you know, salt of the earth kind of thing, our working-class background to form like a raft across the lake of eggnog, and I will be Becky and she will be Huck Finn and where oh where is Jim. I ask her if she knows my nephew Ernie, the one we used to call "the fat boy," the one who always wanted to be an engineer, who waved at passing trains from my aunt's backyard. I tell her how he knew all the brakemen by name, they tooted a special hello, and how Ernie eventually followed his dream, how few people do, and he lost all this weight and now he drives for the Southern Pacific. I can see him with a little red bandanna, but I see him roly-poly, not his new svelte self, and with the reports we hear of him I wonder if he might be gay, and doesn't she see, that's another link, his gayness, our gayness. We should raise a glass to him right here and now, but of course he must be closeted as she has to be, the railroads no gay mecca as far as I can tell.

While I'm telling her all this she's not saying a thing. Maybe she's embarrassed. In this group of professionals—one veterinarian, one nurse practitioner, one social worker—a trade job might suggest a lower level of intelligence. But doesn't she see, I have felt this too, as a truckdriver have had women look at my muscles instead of my mouth, as if to suggest if one works the other can't.

I offer her some eggnog, watch to see if the hori-

30

zon lightens on her face. For some unknown reason something shifts. She softens.

I ask, "Now tell me, I really want to know. What is it you do on the railroad?"

"I *do* the books."

The evening goes on as evenings will. I sneak into the guest room for a little breather, to right myself again, and after a while return with the *Cosmopolitan Magazine Bedside Astrologer,* always a crowd-pleaser. I say complimentary things about Taurus, her sign, though it's one of my least favorite signs, nothing personal, just that she's earth and I'm air and there lies the rub.

The point is I win her back. She ribs me and I rib her and her girlfriend comes into the picture, a woman who could be an aunt of mine, who looks a lot like Ernie's mother, masculine and beautiful with gray hair cropped close at the temple and then longer in back. I have seen a million dykes like her, obvious dykes, immediately apparent to any of us in the congregation. She grabs the railroad woman around the waist, jumps into the conversation, stakes her claim. Starts telling me about their upcoming plans, how dykes will if they think there's some flirting going on. (Once a woman told me about the puppy she and her girlfriend—whom I had designs on—were getting, implying that with the new addition there'd be no extracurricular hanky-panky, no, no time for that with the papers in the kitchen and the dog obedience classes and well, she got her point across.)

But I'm not interested in the railroad woman. I'm just trying to make amends.

This woman, Ernie's mom, is a Gemini, so I think

fast. I tell her about her upcoming year astrology-wise, as I'm a Gemini, too, and I've already memorized our erogenous zones and our amorous days and our color and the music we should play for romantic nights.

I ask them how they met. It feels like a concession, but the question always serves as a good intro, a way dykes can tell their coming out stories. Though it segues into the most intimate of topics, how and when you bed whom you bed, it's the standard question, it's the open door. And here they are wrapped around each other, their bodies entwined in some kind of wedding toast, just begging to tell.

Dot, the older one with the close-cropped hair, starts in. I sit back, get ready for the inevitable, put a smile on. I know better than to risk any other response.

She is working in a mill town, in the mill, somewhere in northern Washington State. She has three kids, the husband gone, divorced or killed or simply left. She goes to the mill every day and punches the clock, does whatever—packs paper, inspects logs—some job with lots of noise around to drown her thoughts.

She is gay. She may have known it forever, suffering through her husband's fumbling attempts, the three children spurted out, her fertile eggs having nothing to do with whether she likes it or not. To look at Dot is to know she has always been a dyke, though there were those years of babies and aiming to please and ignoring that part of herself.

But it gets to be too much—the mill, the grind— and one night (how many nights led to this?) she puts on her white pants suit, the one that shows her off, the one with the white sandals to match, and drives down to Kelso, seventy-five miles away, where there is a gay bar called The Hut. She makes a deal with herself as the miles pass. If there's a parking space open in front of the tavern, she will park and go in.

As fate would have it (and how else can you figure?), someone inside the bar picks the next moment to have a fight, to say things that shouldn't be said, and then, squealing out of the lot, leaves that one space open for Dot. There are those who believe this is all mapped out, the seed of the argument, the tire tracks, the green lights Dot hits as she drives into town.

Dot pulls in, leaves her foot on the brake so the red lights continue to shine though the car is parked, feels her fingers on the metal of the door handle, and then finally her white sandals on the wet pavement of the lot.

Inside, the place is packed. She walks over to a table, one not too far from the door, sits down and orders a Coke from the waitress with long curls, searches her eyes for a sign of recognition. It's happy hour and the waitress, who has a lot of orders to fill, who's been saving for a pair of lizard-skin boots, takes the order without so much as a smile, knowing a Coke will bring only a small tip.

Dot gets her drink in no blink of an eye. There's music on. Patsy Cline and then some disco and she can't tell, it all sounds alike. She doesn't look like anyone here, everyone in blue jeans and tank tops, feels people notice this, feels hot, like a spotlight is being trained on her. Feels as if she's being singled out.

Across the room, fresh in from a day at the station, Millie has been watching and can't seem to get this woman's story. The woman in white grips the Coke like someone would grip an ax handle. With that kind of strength. There's no way anyone is going to be able to pry those fingers loose.

Two younger women sit down at the woman's table and though they're not talking to the lady in white, Millie figures they're her daughters. Maybe she's a mother and has come as their chaperone, to case the joint, to see if it's okay. All that would be fine and good but there's no interaction between mother and brood, and the two young ones, after listening to some songs and playing footsie under the table, head for the door. Now what?

Then (who pushes her to do it? what else is at work?) Millie gets up, goes over, says what comes first: "You're the most scared-looking person I've ever seen."

Maybe she says it like a compliment. Maybe she says it with a tone of awe. Either way, it isn't the regular opening line. Dot looks up, frightened and relieved that someone has offered this door.

"I'm down here seeing if there's some *funny* people left in the world."

"Oh, honey, we're *all* funny down here."

They laugh. Dot feels a space open around her, as if her arms and legs can suddenly stretch. Millie asks her to wait, goes over to the bar where she gets some phone numbers—a gay help-line, a lesbians-in-transition group—and brings them back, explains there's always ways to get involved. Then one of those silent moments comes. The space closes, shrinks up. Millie excuses herself and begins playing pool.

Once the rhythm of expand and contract gets going, once there's been that range of motion, nothing stays the same. Millie hits the pockets, but all the while there is this set of eyes on her every move and she, in turn, moves differently. Posing and pool do go together. You draw out that arm on the beautiful green felt background, you hitch up your hips a bit, and it all suggests other positions. It takes you out of your normal pattern of movement.

(I break in, turn and ask Millie if that's what did it, her pool expertise. "She liked the way my fanny moved in those jeans," she offers. At this Dot blushes, turns red, like someone has their foot on the brake and won't let up.)

At two in the morning Millie's pool buddies go home. The waitress, who has made enough on tips to buy the left boot but not the right, is in a bad mood and wants to close up. Millie suggests to Dot they go for coffee and that's what they do, finding a Denny's open—Denny's, the house of foreplay, the scene of so many prebedding arrangements.

Millie, who is in the Sierra Club and recycles the tiniest thing, quizzes Dot over the Cremora packet, knows she can't go to bed with someone who believes in clear-cutting. Somehow she brings this in and Dot starts talking about growing up in the Northwest, remembers what she hasn't remembered in years—her love of the trees, the slick feel of moss—says all she cannot say with the buzz saws going and ends with, "I guess that makes me an environmentalist too." It's then Millie suggests a hike.

They drive up to a ridge. It's another test but Dot passes, her white sandals covered with dirt, mud spotting the straps. The moon is out and the trees are stand-

35

ing still and they don't kiss then but do the next time they meet. After that it takes a couple months to pack up her life, to disengage, but finally Dot uproots, Dot moves down, and together they set up housekeeping. They bank on a future.

Both of them sit back. They've just relived it, they see nothing else. Their union is in the air, expands outward, as if their lives can finally breathe. I move my chair back to give them some room, to edge the others away, and suddenly want to bronze those white sandals, to make a trophy to their love.

After a moment the room comes back into focus. There is more mingling and talk, all the chatter that usually happens when you get thirty women in a room. One woman goes to the piano and begins to plink out "Silent Night." I look over to where Millie and Dot are sitting—playing pool without the pool table—watch them sing "Silent Night" to each other like it's a love song, like that was the song's original purpose. Someone asks for a secular song, any secular song, and with that people begin to sing show tunes. I offer up "It's A Sin To Tell A Lie," and the rest join in like it's an anthem.

At the end of the evening the railroad woman gives me a firm handshake, no harm done, as if we've really been through it together. I wish her and her girlfriend well, use the words *you both* six times. They climb into Millie's pickup and start it up. The driveway is covered with ice and snow and the truck fishtails over the road's surface. A minute later all I can see are the brake lights signaling back, two swaying red lanterns on the track.

TWO

Loaves And Fishes

He steers his boat to a spot where he's been lucky before, where the pattern of the waves hints at something below. Where he has a feeling. Shapes call to him as they called to his father and his father's father, a high inaudible sound, pitched far above human ears.

Here he lays out his nets like tablecloths draping the sea, as his wife would lay a table, setting it, and after the nets are cast he waits, as she waits. Their life together is about this waiting. He wanders and she reels him in. He thinks of her then, how she makes do when they have nothing, finding food in an empty pantry, *her belief in him, some miracle performed.*

By late afternoon he's finished the task. He leaves the nets out overnight to move in the currents, to tangle and unwind, *her hair on the pillow,* in the sea below.

He does not see it coming, the prow of a rival boat around the bend. Before he can signal, the boats circle, at each other like two dogs in a yard. Before he can cry out, the other boat changes course, passing over his wake. He hears what he thinks to be cries, or perhaps it is the churning, the wake now throwing off lengths of twine, roped brown tendrils swaying in the current. And then, as when upon awakening he had felt the shapes in the net, the dark mass of them below the surface, he feels their going *(as she always senses his going before he leaves),* and the catch is released into the surrounding sea.

He turns, walks into the galley, and comes back with a packaged loaf of bread. He draws his arm back as if to throw a punch but instead throws the loaf in their direction, the open end of the bread spilling out white squares onto the sea. "You take the food off my wife's table, out of my children's mouths. Take this and eat it, all of you."

The white bread floats, and he sees the fish rise, partake of the feast, *the meal she has prepared,* before gulls come and pirate what is left away.

SMELT

He is off somewhere with other fishermen on
the dock. Bullshitting about the season, quotas,
about Alaska. I collect pieces of twine, stray
bits left over where men were mending the nets.
Earlier I watched as they sewed the holes a
dolphin or shark had torn.

I tie the pieces together in a long line, the
way convicts tie sheets together to lower their
bodies down, and then hook a safety pin on the end
with a torn piece of bologna found in the galley,
the meat already beginning to turn gray around
the edges. The fish won't know the difference.

In my dreams fish are pulled up hand over fist.
I haul them in, their silver bodies with a hint
of twitch, a satisfied look on their faces, this
last bite of sandwich a last supper. The fish
always take what I offer, satisfied with the gift.

Over the edge, too near the edge (where is the
hand to stop me, where is the warning voice) I
drop the line, watch the pin pierce the water
and wait. I lift the hook out again and again.
The bait comes up unaltered, no tear, no telling
mark. When he returns I have nothing to show. We
climb into the Jeep, the sun cutting out a section
of sky like a round hole in the netting for us
to escape through.

Once he and I went out at night, just the two of us.
With hooks placed at intervals on the wire, every
inch or so, we watched glints of metal disappear
into the black water below. Soon the poles began
to hum. In the moonlight, the smelt came up like
Christmas bells on the line of hooks, each bell
attached and ringing.

BOTTLES

I know he's tossing one down.
I know. I can tell.
I know he's tossing one down.

He'd finish a bottle (lips to sleeve, release), walk
across the kitchen floor, heavy-footed, black-mark
the linoleum, and opening the door leading to the garage
stand on the step, stock-still. With enough heft (his
aim suddenly accurate) so the bottle would not shatter,
he sent it through the air and it fell on top of the
others, the cry of glass in the cardboard box.

Upended, drops trickled out and wet the cardboard,
turned it mushy, no longer square, no more right
angles, the brown sides becoming round and soft,
limp as his stare.

When the box was full he'd take it in his big hands
(hands that had cradled the bottle, hands that had
cradled my hands) and together we'd put it in the Jeep
and drive down to the pier, the cries of glass louder
now as the bottles rearranged themselves in the box.

There, near the edge, we laughed and we laughed as we
stood, tossing them, one by one, off the dock. Tossing
another and then another. Tossing another one down.

TROUT

We take the old road. I know the spots where
the hills let loose a slim line of waterfall.
The cooked shrimp stands. The place where we
can get a piece of pie on the way back.

I take my eyes from the windshield and watch
him drive, his hands steady on the wheel like
when he steers the boat out of the harbor. He
stares at the horizon, the cigar in his mouth
a divining rod giving us direction.

We turn off and I look for a sign, a clue to mark
the spot. There is only the common blanket of
evergreens. A dirt road. Ruts with no discernible
pattern. Behind us the gray highway continuing.
With nothing outstanding, memory will never take
hold. We pull alongside a river and get out of
the Jeep.

We are quiet for a while. Every couple of seconds
a trout jumps up, twists its backbone into an S
and then plops down, the river already having carried
on, the fish landing in a different spot. I think
about the trout farm, crammed with black shapes, inky
bodies of fish changing the water, making it thick
as mud.

The sky is like the background of a painting I have
seen in school, a scene of Washington crossing the

Delaware. Washington stands in the boat with his
chest out, full of himself, looking over the bow.
The sky is his backdrop, painted in a way that lets
you know it's a momentous occasion.

This sky gives no clues. I can't commit a section
of it to memory, have it stay the same, be there on
my return. I look at the river one last time. We
climb back into the Jeep, heading for the old highway
again. He pumps the brakes and they catch, just past
the stop sign.

INK FISH

We gather around his latest gift, turn our noses at the smell. Taking what is offered she moves to the cutting board, has learned early on to gut salmon, perch, halibut, cod. Here is the arrangement. She will cook what he brings in.

A gray mess spills out as the newspaper opens, squid the metal color of the sea when the day is overcast, a gray weather that depresses her. She takes the good knife, first slices the heads off, then down one side to open them up. Freed of form the squid slip through her fingers, evade her grasp, elusive as a husband drawn by the sea.

She slides out the dark sack of intestines, the squid marks her, her hands now black with ink. We dance around the kitchen, yell *inkfish inkfish,* the only name we've ever known. If we took fountain pens, placed them in the mouth of the squid, pulled the hammer back, we could fill up each cartridge with secrets of the sea.

Their bodies lie flat on the newsprint like dull sheets left hanging on the line to dry. Their wetness alters the print. Every story blurs.

This is what he tells us. There are nights when a grayness enters his bones, a grayness that depresses. It's then he bends over the bow, called, as he is always called, to look deep into the waves. Then he sees us: this image at the table, his wife inside a circle, his family gathered round. When he misses her he sees her dark form in the waves.

She skims off what is left of ocean, the slickness, then pounds them tender. We hear each squid slap the board, see the small dents the knife handle makes. She readies the pan, tosses them in. With the slightest heat they curl, turn opaque. Nothing is ever clear. At the sink she rinses off her hands. The ink goes down the drain. A story finds its way back to the sea.

The History Of Fabric

My mother never

>moved far enough, or moved too far,
from tract to brick,
rental to claim,
years of scrimp and save,
finally, oh finally, the camel coats,
the roughshod husband in subtle tweed,
who could then deny her
the heft of midweight cotton, the truth
of dotted swiss, no sign
as telling to signal
distance   from where she

>returned after he died, back
down the ladder, the loss
of brim, the beginning of fray,
now, close the eyes upon her,
close the prying eyes.
At night the neighbors circled round
in sweaters pilled and sagging,
in telling woolen vests,
while above the moon, unbleached
sang soft

>oh the loss of tartan
oh the days of plaid.

STEUBEN

We ride up the escalator, marking our distance
from the basement, the sale floor, the seconds,
climbing up and out, past women's wear, linen,
china, recite the names: Wedgwood, Waterford,
Beleek, the trademark small green clover on
the thin lip of each cup.

The Steuben glass room is set off from the rest
of the floor, we cross some dividing line, breathe
shallow, the air somehow thinner, enter a dark
blue cave with glass shelves lit from beneath,
on each a piece of crystal floating.

Making our way around the perimeter, we pay
homage, the neo-Grecian vase, the small "affordable"
animals, a bear, a cat, price tags make us swoon,
each piece a world we fall into without shatter,
feel the breath of the salesperson near, his
"Can I help you?" like a slap.

One vase has an etching inside the glass, a forest
scene, willows bending white in an unseen wind.
Looking closer I see our faces reflected, the
small o's our mouths make, my mother beaming,
her three daughters refracted into a benevolent
future, some better standing in the world.

We drive home, us three in the back with Mom as
chauffeur. Opening the front door we hurt our
eyes on the candy dish, the orange Depression glass
holding common dinner mints. I run out, with my
sisters' pooled resources, to buy a cake pedestal
I've seen at Woolworth's made of glass—ornate,
classy, meant to hold something up.

All of us gather around, hold our breath, the air
somehow thinner now, watch her take it out of the
box, realize too late. In the kitchen light even
I can see the flaw in the design, the thick, chunky
base, the terrifying trim.

PINK HARVEST

She stands at the kitchen window, fillets the salmon, slices a straight line down the belly of the fish. She could do this in her sleep. Outside the window the sky is full of red clouds, the kind that appear only in winter. *Red sky in the morning, sailor take warning. Red sky at night, sailor's delight.* Since it's afternoon she breathes a sigh of relief.

The front door opens. He comes in, plants a kiss, longer than usual, then throws a fat package on the drainboard. She picks up the package to weigh it, her hands accurate scales, figures she's dealing with three pounds of something. Without further ceremony tosses off the newsprint. Inside, a mound of pure pink fans out, the color so vivid it takes a moment for her eyes to adjust. She looks closer. The shrimp become distinct, individual. Some lie hooked together, entwined, a baby's finger curled around the mother's. "Take a good look," he says, "pink harvest of the sea."

He starts in, tries to sell her on a new gamble. As if her whole life with him isn't one. Someone has gotten hold of his ear, convinced him of money to be earned fishing shrimp instead of salmon, the salmon he has spent a lifetime tracking. He reaches down, scoops some up, the shrimp dripping through his fingers. He believes in the possibility of a big return, can picture his hands plowing through piles of money, green bills floating through the air. She notices how small the shrimp are. So pink. So feminine. How they drift down like petals. How can he risk their economic future on something so delicate?

He asks her to look at this a different way. He tells her to let her eyes drift, adjust her sights downward. He tells her the bottom of the sea is pink.

He will illustrate his point. Outside the kitchen window the sky is red. The sea will be calm tomorrow, something she knows to be true. He builds on that, predicts a glowing future, says the sky is a reflection—not of the sunset—but of what lies below the waves.

There is no hindsight at the start of a journey, no indication of outcome. All we have is what we can conjure. She turns back to the cutting board, tries to think: how the color of the sky can influence the water, how the bottom of the ocean can influence the sky.

What The Tetas Promise

We tumble into the sedan, three laps in front, five in back, one sister, the quiet one, perched on a set of knees, loaded up past the limit, each dip, bump, throws us closer to the ceiling. Before long the sign City Limits, then tracks, right side, wrong side, and we strain necks to see down the line, the small fires hobos make, while the *tetas** put on the gas. The town behind us, we drive into fields, scent of dirt, gas, and blossom through the car windows opened wide, the air laden.

What the *tetas* promise: cherries, black tubs full; trees heavy with their own weight, bowing branches down within arm's reach. A guarantee our small hands will be filled.

When the car stops, clouds of dust. We spill out and someone gets buckets and someone gets sacks and we race into the orchard where there are rows and order. Ladders lean against trees we cannot climb, the *tetas'* warning voices, but never mind, this is now a merry-go-round, the golden rings plump and dark red and we grab and grab and grab, lightening the load of the tree. Each branch lifts, weight shed, and cherries ping in the bucket or into mouths, stain everywhere.

The quiet sister picks only the best, only the most perfect, no peck or flaw, as how in kindergarten she cut along the paper doll line (the fat scissors unwieldy, small handles cut into skin) then slipped outside the line, crying. We will never be able to lighten her load. She has an

---

Aunts in Croatian

53

eye for beauty, can see the cherries in a bowl, placed, while the rest of us could care, don't care, smash and throw the cherries, direct hit. The *tetas* laugh, plop one or two in their mouths as they pick, roll them from side to side to side with their tongues. We can see the shape of the cherry in their puffed-out cheeks and someone grabs the side of one *teta*'s face and juice spits out.

When we've had enough the *tetas* gather the bushel of us, call us to the weigh station at the edge of the field, where a scale swings slightly, a round globe, next to a dark green truck. A man is there, indistinct, just his outline like a palm in the sunset, just his form to give us measure. Only when we're right on top of him do we see round bumps on his face, in a row, along the jaw, a long red ridge like a soft mountain range laid on his face or under his skin so that this face is not a face but a topographic map, ridges and plains, as when we painted plaster-of-paris models of the country in school, the Mississippi and then west, rising to the Rockies and back down to the San Fernando Valley. "Tumors," one *teta* says to the other in a hush, and "Don't eat," the other *teta* turns and says to us as he takes the cherries, dumps them onto the scale and then back into a bag that looks used and crumpled, and then hands them back to us.

We strain necks to see, how these bumps bow down one side of his face, within reach, the skin covering but not covering, as if he is puffing up his cheek. He goes on breathing and talking the price of cherries, the *tetas* nodding along, but everything has gone out of them and they are stiff now, no sweet evening breezes.

No one says a word as cherries fall, dropped from the sack or thrown from the car window like small red worlds, the front seat quiet now as we move along. Soon it will be evening, orange sky and black palms, somewhere a mariachi winding down or faint through the tinny radio. We watch the radio dial grow in vibrant light inside, as outside the light begins to fade.

In a corner of the car the silent one rocks from side to side to side. We watch the *tetas* watch her, see the truth register: laden, she is laden. They will never cleanse this stain. The last sun reflects off the dash, paints hands and faces red. The *tetas* do what they must do. They carry us home.

Where You Go For Comfort

1.

Late at night inside your room:

> not into the past, to hearth, mother, night-light
> in the hall, no doting one, a grandma, kitchen
> lamp and something from the oven, the art of care,
> or quiet strength, what men were, the arms of the
> fireman who lifted you, age five, and took you from
> your burning house, your crib, and Augie Doggie
> going up in smoke.

> nor into the present, a cozy room, books, friends
> gathered round, willing to tell you all you are
> is good. The one you love would try to fix things,
> distract. She doesn't know where you go when you
> are like this.

2.

Seated at your desk, you take a book down, a life ring,
and read:

> "...his own identity was fading out into the grey
> impalpable world: the solid world itself which
> these dead had one time reared and lived in was
> dissolving and dwindling."

You forgot it was this easy, this safe, to slip away, and
every time you tried to ask for help, the effort caught

you. The computer screen lies black before you, the black blank screen, slashes of white where once the cursive rolled and rolled. You read on:

"...softly falling into the dark mutinous Shannon Waves..."

and this is close, the entry. You ride it out,this image, until you're on the sea.

3.

The crew sleeps below. The captain is gone. You take the helm, like your father taught you. The fathometer's broken (what folly to think we'd ever know depth) though for a moment a soft green light comes from the dial, the first invitation, sea-green. The ship to shore is on but useless. Where there was life now there's only static, some last attempt to tell them that you loved them, but then again that never worked.

Here nothing ties. Out there, in the center of the ocean, the sky black, sea-black, the only light may be from a star, a night-light in the hall. Everything is fictional, your life to this point. One look at the waves and you go under. This is what you came for, but you needn't worry. There is no boat, no structure. You haven't a body now so there's no turmoil in the rolling, roiling waves. You slip in, where you go for comfort, here in this study, your dark room on the sea.

from *Dubliners* ("The Dead") by James Joyce

THREE

...when the lights of health go down, the undiscovered countries that are disclosed...

Virginia Woolf, "On Being Ill"

Auto Body

My mother brings her car in, needle on the red, explains: "It's never gone on the red before." At the garage the mechanic says, "Ma'am," he says, "Ma'am, it may take thousands of dollars to fix this, it may take thousands, let me take it off your hands." She hands it over, gives him the car, damage can't be turned back.

When all you cling to rots, every board gives way, wood damp at the center, unable to bear your weight (though you've grown so thin), the question becomes one of measurement, how to estimate loss. In the nursing journal they describe your body as a "far from equilibrium system."

When she calls from a pay phone, tells me the story, after the fact, I call him an evil son of a bitch. Then stop, qualify, "Maybe evil's not right." Then feel this is a dodge. "Evil as it equates to hell."

When everything conspired, planned elsewhere, needle on the red when the mercury went up, I could not move my legs, I could not move my arms, the illness a force I was no match for. The mechanic is a force she is no match for. Is that not evil?

Two weeks later we learn he's turned around and sold the car for twice its value, made a tidy profit. I tell her we should haul him in, get the authorities involved. But she'll have none of this, remembering the car's betrayal. Says, "I couldn't count on it. This is for the best." As if the mechanic were heaven-sent, as if this were meant to be.

When you have been betrayed by your body in
the early years, in your prime, there is no
sense, all is teeter, everything is uncertain:
the postman's arrival, the due date of books,
your lover's promise—though she is reputable,
though she has seen you through—yes, even she
is suspect and there is

nothing to count on (as if you could count,
as if you could remember sequence or why we use
numbers), there is no greater system, no scheme
of order, far from equilibrium, far from home

you take the dime anyway, Mother always said
you should, you take the dime in case of trouble,
in case you need to call.

How To Use The Sick

You tell us
with our mouths clamped down
around the mercury that soars
we drain your coffers, need too much
require research, softened touch
we waste away and worry you

We've never truly pulled our weight
as shut-ins with no place to go
in houses hot with fetid steam
our purple flowers lose their form

Longing then to be of use
not left to linger in our beds
dampen wet the sallow sheets
with all that good heat gone to waste

It's now come time to harvest this
It's time to learn to use the sick

We're at the ready, move us round
wherever there's the slightest chill
given chance to earn our keep
we won't complain, we'll just put out

Place us in your shivered fields
staggered there amid the rows
hang us swinging in your groves
let our fevers so assure
that juice on every table flows

Like smudgepots prop us up at will
by broccoli and grapefruit found
near kale and beets in frozen ground
tomatoes green in frigid climes
could benefit from being close
turn red like rage that inks your cheeks
your tundra heart's a tougher thaw

So let our fevers heat the fields
killer frost we will beat back
with arms and legs and vents in place
your glow worms, baby burners blow

It's way past time to harvest this
It's way past time to use the sick.

Inventory

1. one spot aching, on the left upper arm, as if
   a thumb pressed and stayed, drilled into the center.
   A maiden aunt holds the cheek a second too long. (If
   this the existence of phantom pain, what then has
   been cut? Some donut hole in the center of the
   bicep.)

2. or lying on the left side, or the right, forgetting
   distinction. (She pens an *L*, an *R* on her shoes, fat
   laces pulled through eyelets in kindergarten, learns
   to tie.)

3. blazes, everywhere blazes.

4. an irregular heartbeat, John Cage in a snit,
   a call to attention, like taps or reveille, the rest
   of the body up now, erect, listening for a metrical
   pattern gone awry.

5. lost and found; synapses require a sender, a
   receiver. Oil the mitt. The ball arcs, then sputniks
   off course. How long will you wait, hope in your
   throat, for it to come down? Could you even see it
   now, at twilight, white spots that continue to flash
   above?

6. What's the hypothalamus up to?

7. identities (plural) you cannot retrieve. (Who
   you once were appears on a milk carton with a number
   to call: What was she wearing? Which name will she
   answer to?)

8. If she knew *duration*, she'd have packed differently.

9. an affable death, your own holy notion.

10. cracking, bones cracking.
    clichés—if remembered—provide history, anchor.
    what do bones do:
    > knit
    > break
    > set (if left too long on the line to dry).

11. referred pain: "How'd you hear about us?"

12. a field of vision adjusts downward, an economy
    on the skids, or a spiral circling into a drain at
    the end of the cartoon. Darkness at the four corners.
    On the periphery cease to exist: cars, special
    interests, errant dogs. Let someone else chase them.

PILGRIMAGE

I travel to Arizona in a rented beige Taurus,
aerodynamically designed, the fenders of the car
soft and curved, take my sick body, this tired
package, to the identified vortex. I'm on a
pilgrimage, without the bonnets and big-buckled
shoes of Plymouth Rock, without the bowing east
or west, though one thing's similar: I'm ready
to go to extremes.

Sedona is ringed in tall red cathedrals of stone
which on certain days sport Camaros and Firebirds,
cars lifted there by cranes for ad campaigns,
gravity defied. Driving into the area I likewise
feel a pull, that delicious tug, like a vacuum-
cleaner tube placed against the palm, know I'm
on to something.

I need coffee to keep my balance, not quite ready
to give over will or belief, find a place called
the Croissant Shack tucked into a back courtyard,
no one but me and a dark-haired woman taking flaky
things out of the oven. Even they swirl.

I order up a cup. She looks into my eyes, says,
"You've been in pain a long time," this after
making change for a five. She is right about
me but wrong about croissants—heavy, leaden,
but by now it's clear the shack is a cover like
the man who sells drugs from the ice-cream cart
back home.

She talks like she's Moses dressed in priestly robes,
a blue-striped apron with BISTRO across the front,
tells me I've come to the right place, there are
healing rocks down by the river. I need only go
there and lie down (which is all I've wanted from
the start).

Following her map, penned on the back of a flyer
advertising a breakfast special, I drive down to a
park on the edge of town. There a boy-meets-girl
ritual is going on. Supple teenage bodies drink
beer without caution, without crystals or crusts
to weigh them down. A ritual's a ritual. I, too,
have brought along a six-pack, just in case.

Everything pulls the body down. I slog through
shallow water, head for the hollowed-out places
along the bank where the stream swirls out over
red earth. The rock surface is flat, red, warm.
I lie down on the back of someone, that is how it
feels, soft, curved, the hard edges worn away,
feel buoyed by stone.

Before coming to Sedona the croissant woman worked
in an electronics plant in Marin. One day she was
called to the Southwest. I know some similar
decision needs to be made, a final giving over.
I take another pull from the bottle. What happened
to the anxious pilgrims who felt the world was flat,
who wanted to turn back? The pilgrims who were
there to witness the sight of falls at the horizon's
edge?

LIFE AFTER WESTERN MEDICINE
(SHE TRIES ANOTHER APPROACH)

for Robert

Everything flows out, he says,
like a faucet turned on and then,
with the ring of the phone, forgotten,
there is no stopper,
everything goes, a barn burner,
a white sale.
What others replenish (the life force, energy)—
the way stone fountains
bring forth a steady stream from the statue's breast—
flows through you to the ground.

He draws a picture on a piece of paper,
my body in stick form: head, eyes,
arms, breasts, torso,
then, with a great flurry of scratches, pen on paper,
a wellspring from heart and loins,
a Niagara spilling out, a busted main.

He says it all has something to do with
pockets of grief, thousands of years old,
not a one-hanky matinee,
a welling up, some sorrow that cannot be stemmed.
I think of every leaving:
each time my father went to sea
or when my husband slept with the girl next door,
and every slight puncture of the heart,
now a colander, a sieve.

He asks me to lie down
then places his hands over the spots,
as if to solder. I feel a heat, then
movement, a shift of an underground
stream, watch him turn the flood back,
like Superman bending steel rods into a U shape,
or the TVA reconstructing the valley floor,
a geography altered.

I get up, thank him for his time.
That night, at home, readying for bed,
I unbutton my ill-fitting blouse,
find flowers in full bloom,
a forest, heather, potted palms,
a living diorama across my middle,
fed by some unseen eternal spring.

BREAD-AND-BUTTER NOTE

The small things apply. A note for the book. Some response to say it meant a lot, you noticed the effort, you're still with the world.

So you select a card from the pile you keep in a drawer, the first decision—blank or printed, the over-used Hoppers or the opium flowers or the Frankenthaler card you've been saving for someone special—and you place in a note, a thank you, something penned as if off-the-cuff, airy jottings, but each small word counted, weighed all the way to *yours truly* or *with affection* or the wide-distanced *sincerely,* the name signed once then thrown out, how the end letter dipped too low, indicated something not right (you don't want to weigh her down). Another penned, the right lilt this time, then stamped, sealed, all of that activity. Odd what has become effort.

Carrying it from desk to the telephone stand beside the door, placing it there, you imagine its journey, hearing that just this morning they arrested a postal worker who had squirreled away thousands of letters in his apartment because he was exhausted, couldn't keep up with the work. You think of bags of letters filling his room, no room to breathe, then remember the story of the woman with hundreds of cats in her small studio, all of them pressing in on her, all the crying voices, so many that she had a bed constructed in the center of the room covered in chicken wire, the one place she had to get away.

Looking at the letter again you notice something's wrong, it's incomplete, a wide plain of white where the street address should be. You think it's Pine or Spruce or maybe a deciduous tree, you can't be certain, you're less sure of so many things, so you search for the address book, something you haven't picked up in days. Once in hand there's that cavalcade of names, all those letters, *a* and *b*, and C., whom you never called, she sick with cancer and you not calling, the last time you saw her she was wizened away and if you don't call soon there will be less of her, less of her, fewer pills in the bottle, another reminder that the gamma globulin bottle is low, *your* love potion #9, what you shoot in to give you energy. Funny how it doesn't seem to be doing its job, the stuff in you but you cannot track it, deposited in some dead-letter office, otherwise the book wouldn't feel so heavy in your hands, the weight of it, all the calls you haven't made. You quickly find the right name, the right street, but not before lifting the phone (who can lift you), cordless you must wait, the small indecision before the dial tone, then hang up when the machine comes on. It is like this, don't you see, each measured movement and what will it cost, each page calling out, first a trio, then a quartet, and then the community chorus, all the crying voices, and the only thing that saves you, the one thing you have done, is to put the address down, it's ready to go, the small things apply, you have sent your bread-and-butter note.

Before Daily Care Strikes

[Agnes] Martin has said that her paintings "are about freedom from the cares of this world," and that they are meant to help people "before daily care strikes."

Holland Cotter, *Agnes Martin: All The Way To Heaven*

Maybe there is a color, a slim band, between the dream with all its activities, and the first waking, when what was running on yesterday's screen resumes, uninterrupted, the bad blood of the day before is bad blood again. But before you start, in bed, before daily care strikes, weights you down as you dray yourself up, pulling workhorse, the human body a thick red cord (Who will strum the string taut? Which demon, which evil, bad sister will pluck and pluck and pluck?) Before daily care strikes there is something I cannot remember. If I feel into color, inch my fingers in, can I stay—pinked salmon, sea-green—if I fell in, was left alone? Edge care out of the room, sweep the corners clean, pretend there is no day, no headlong battle, your neighbor Mrs. A., incapacitated, decapitated, her head a hubcap rolling down the road after the crash. Before daily care strikes is there music, before the radio alarm is there heartache? Look to the sky outside for color that will throw you. Strike, strike, strike up the band of blue, then pink, then there, where they mix, head over heels, fall.

What Helen Knows

On the first of each month she goes to the newsstand,
takes magazines from the shelf, *Bazaar, Cosmopolitan,
Mademoiselle,* magazines that, given her looks (lesbian,
feminist, big-belted, non-nyloned) don't quite fit.
Other customers glance over, uneasy, a spy gaining secrets
from the enemy camp, which tip is she picking up?

She flips past the table of contents, the ad pages, a
model in a thong bikini, the scent of Obsession hits the
man standing next to her with his face in *Monster Trucks,*
the mix frightening, surf and turf, she thumbs furiously,
in fear of being caught with her nose between Coco Chanel
and the do's and don'ts of fashion.

She's been going to this source for years, on the sly, off-
hours, when friends are otherwise engaged, skips articles
on how to achieve multiple orgasms (if it's good, isn't
one enough?), ways to make your apartment *spicy,* your
appearance *saucy,* familiar now with the cast of
characters, Helen Gurley Brown, who's kept her man, her
David, happy

with so many goddamned tricks the guy must be exhausted,
"doing research" (as if Helen were there during coitus with
abacus in hand, counting, counting), Helen's been nipped,
tucked, and rolled like a '57 Chevy, well-preserved, but
one thing's for certain, Helen looks happy, Helen looks
engaged and it follows: How does she keep it up, what
does Helen know?

Turning to the astroscope, she locates her sign, wants a
clue, she wants a clue, dammit. There, in black and white
she reads of her *quicksilver allure,* that she is *madcap,*
feckless, words she would never use let alone use to
describe herself, there's talk of *cavorting* (when did she
last cavort?), of *conquest,* and she thinks of Vasco de
Gama, the Sea of Cortez, then of the woman at her office
with the bedroom eyes.

She holds close to the promise of certain lucky days,
March 6th, the full moon on the 12th, the month takes
form, her life takes form, yes, no doubt about it—her
star is on the rise. She closes the cover. Walking out
of the store with new *verve,* with genuine *élan,* as assured
as Helen must be, there is comfort in the knowledge that

big changes will be coming soon.

Dog Tales

"What kind?" people ask, as if this is the most important consideration. What's the difference, I always think. Maybe it says something about society, how people have gotten so breed-specific. But my lover, game for the discussion, produces names and tries out the sound of them: Portuguese water dogs, borzois, English setters, Rhodesian ridgebacks, Belgian sheepdogs. Somehow each name suggests a larger geographic circle, an expanded life.

We are considering getting a dog. This is a big step, bigger than buying the couch, a decision we fought over for three months, settling for some white macrame-type thing that we left on the sidewalk after the last apartment. Somehow couches—like people—can get left, but dogs can't. People with dogs look happy, and our lives have had a few rough turns. Bouts of ill health, a couple of breakups. The specter of *the end* just around the corner. We both have the hope unexpressed: maybe this will turn the tide.

Each of us has, in fact, been in relationships where there was dog-leaving, have told these stories after too many drinks, confessionally mushy, a test of some sort. It's as if by hearing the story the other will really know the bad side of love gone wrong. If they stay after this, you think, they will really stay.

For Sally it was worse. Her ex—who claimed primary ownership of the dog—wouldn't let Sally keep their Brittany in the divorce, though the ex wouldn't keep the dog either. To this day, Hoover lives on a Southern farm hundreds of miles away, across the continent, getting some good old boy's affection on the front seat of a beat-up truck. Sally never forgave the ex, and this is what we both know: you can forgive the ex for cruelty and ignorance and bad judgment, for not loving you enough or loving you too much, but never for what they did to the dog.

We have a system: sixty percent/forty percent. She can have the controlling share.

"An Australian-shepherd cross, twenty dollars!" "A German shorthaired mix!" Each day starts with the pet section in the paper, Sally calling out the line up. There are rescue services for certain breeds. I get roped in and find myself answering the return calls. The rescuers talk in hushed voices, as if they're the resistance forces, the dogs having barely escaped captivity, taken to safety over state lines. The services want to know everything about us. Economics, personal things. *Is your yard fenced? How many hours a day are you home?* I start to resent this, as if we aren't good people. Who *would* contact rescue services—abusers, poisoners, doggiephiles? I mean, if you're willing to take what they've got, no questions asked, doesn't that say something about you as a person?

One woman asked about our security system, square footage, all the specifications, things I would never tell a burglar. One wanted to come the next day for an on-site visit to interview us. I spent the night in a cleaning frenzy, putting out the good bath towels, table linens, our two pieces of real china. What could I do to impress: *Wild Kingdom* tapes? Home-baked snacks in the shape of hydrants?

"It's just so we can know what to expect," says the rescuer.

Little does she know, she's nailed it, what Sally and I keep circling.

Now, every Wednesday, Sally takes me to the SPCA. Something called Doggie Socialization. The animal behaviorists set aside this time, a controlled environment, for problem dogs to mix. All the damaged dogs with complexes, attacked when young, morose for no reason, abandoned and worse.

I know what she's getting at. Would it still be okay, could we survive even this, a pooch with a depressive personality, no Rover with the slipper in his mouth, instead some shaggy Heathcliff with a razor blade poised at the haunch?

Not only do the dogs physically look like the owners, but there's the stamp of personality as well. Denali, the shy mastiff, is as reticent as Jane in social situations. Eeep as arrogant, Huey as big-hearted.

I wonder what kind of dog we'll make.

We enter the SPCA garage, large as an airplane hangar, cleared of foreign objects, the corrugated door opened wide. There, milling around the entrance, is the regular crowd. A very small woman with a fanny pack that reads *Dog Tired* cradles an even smaller Pekinese cross. Gidget's "mom" is holding forth.

"So we go up to the front porch, it's raining out, you know that downpour last week? And I look down at her and I say, 'Gidget Marie, wipe your feet.'" I notice that Gidget, hip to the show, looks up at that precise moment as if on cue.

"And she looks up, like she hasn't heard a word I've said, like it isn't perfectly clear, looks up, mind you, and says, 'What?' Just like that, in the sweetest voice. 'What?'"

"Gidget Marie said what?" I have to ask. Gidge looks over, as if I have the *human* audacity to question this tale.

"Yep, that's what she said."

I mouth "What?" to Sally but she's already turned away and is deep into it with the sheltie owner, a conversation about doggie protein, lamb meal versus corn.

Once a man told me his hound dog talked to him, whimpered, "I have to go tinkle," growled, "Life sucks," distinct, clear as a bell. He said the dog talked in his sleep and that sometimes he thought their dreams crossed. Those two stuck it through for fourteen years.

I take in the rest of the crew. There's Chas and Renato, the gay men with the wheaten terrier, always dressing Bosco up in small pastel bow ties or little Carmen Miranda outfits the dog endures. Next to them is the man with the Rotty who wears one black glove and ropes the metal leash through his hand like a pair of brass knuckles. There's Harry the Airedale and the little schnauzer named Schotzie and, off in the corner, the most depressed dog I've ever seen, Pepe the papillon.

The couple who owns Pepe comes every week. The story goes that they sent to Wisconsin for him—a rare breed—but that there was something sketchy about his previous home. A dog with a troubled past. They took him anyway.

"He's a real cutup at home," Pepe's mom says. She looks like Mary—of Peter, Paul, and Mary—that same blonde bowl-cut, that same affect.

"The life of every evening," chimes in her husband, but there's a little push to the voice. As if they're trying to sell me on the idea. A lampshade on the head kind of dog.

Pepe skulks around the perimeter, suspicious. *Someone* has beaten this dog.

I wonder about Pepe's people, the investment without a return, the kind of generosity that operates in the face of no immediate gratification. How long can you stick with it, believing the person will finally break through?

When Sunday rolls around Sally says she's taking me on a drive. This is my favorite thing to do so there's no resistance. To get wherever we're going we have to drive to the Piers. Before we know it the street is blocked with a crush of people, tourists who have seen so many San Francisco commercials they must act in love, are forced to be in love. (Not that some of them don't feel it, aren't having some sort of fun, but there's that desperation there, too, as if they're posing with their shrimp cocktail. Each couple hesitates for just a moment, lifting the speared crustacean to their mouths, throws their heads back and laughs at the sky—though you get the sense that in their normal lives they're cement watchers, eyes downward, forward march.)

We get out of there and drive down Bay Street by

the Marina with sailboats in the sunset. I start to sing "Red Sails in the Sunset," but she shuts me up. This is no time for romance, this is serious now. Taking a right off the main thoroughfare we drive some back-route way into the Presidio, the military post that's going public, already a shadow of its former self, already less military, and this is when she spills the beans. She's taking me to the pet cemetery, where I swear I've never been though she is sure she has shown me before.

She takes her eyes off the road and fixes me with a look. "If we can weather this, we can weather anything," she says. Maybe to see the end will help us start.

We park by a barracks-style building and then walk through a sandy lot, heading for some dark passage under a freeway overpass. I can hear the cars overhead and think back about the one dog I had that got hit and limped all its life. These are the kinds of things I'm thinking.

When we come to a small picket-fenced area I can tell it's going to get rough. The pet cemetery is a little too cute, the gravemarkers to Rolf and Jed and Kikki Sue—some references to duty and having lived a noble life. My, how we project onto dogs and cats, as if just by living a conscripted life, knowing the military lawns, the frequent unsettling moves, the absence from master, the animals have lived a life worthy of medals, a purple heart to pin on that stupid Pomeranian's hairy chest. There are graves to UNKNOWN with red hearts stenciled in on white markers. It is the neat and tidy sentiments I have a hard time with, but thank god, no yellow ribbons. As if we might think the ribbon was originally white and young Spot came along and did his certain duty.

I'm upset about something but I don't know what and start to whistle "Bridge on the River Kwai" to lighten things up. She is not amused.

We step gingerly around the little mounds.

"We could get two," she says. "Then it'll help split my affection and I won't get so attached." But this rationale certainly didn't help when we were dating and she was seeing someone else. Who's to say you wouldn't just love twice as much, or the love wouldn't get diluted? Or the more frightening thought: Will either get supplanted?

As we walk along we keep having conversations like this, hedging our bets, protecting ourselves—and I finally realize what it is about dogs. It's the lack of cunning I'm drawn to, no calculations, no subterfuge. How you look at a dog and the love you feel is clear, you both know it, and nothing else needs to be said.

Out of the corner of my eye I see movement over by a corner plot. An old man with a cap, alone, bends over a grave changing the plastic flowers. He stands and gives a final salute.

Tonight it's another Disney movie. She forces me to go. Animals who've endured and triumphed. I'm alright through the first abandonment scene, when the animals get left alone by the family, but when the cat goes over the falls—that's it. I can't bear it, this canine *Terms of Endearment*, these scripted scenes of loss, and I'm crying with the closing credits, and she's holding my head.

Sally walks over to the living room closet, opens the door, and takes down the old family photo albums. We sit together on the couch to page through them. There are scenes of her relatives at picnics, in front of the family stoop. She points to each picture that includes a pet and says, "That dog's dead, that cat's long gone." Just to remind me what I'm in for.

FOUR

VEERING

I got started thinking about characterization. A student asked me—the new writing teacher—for some tips on how to flesh out a character and I gave her a list of questions to ask. But in real life how do you respond to the question: height, weight, age? If a mugger succeeds in grabbing your purse and you get a quick glimpse before being knocked to the pavement, how *do* you tell age? This has particular relevance.

Just last week I was walking in the Marina on one of those terrifically cold days we sometimes get, the wind full of gusts, white caps on the bay, a few hardy souls out "braving it." You had to lean into your step. I was in the homestretch, coming back from having walked out to Fort Point, on that cinder path parallel to Crissey Field, when I saw a man coming toward me, well, not toward me, let's say he was headed in my direction. He was weaving a bit, he did not look purposeful, he was "braving" nothing, acting as if it was seventy degrees, the kind of weather that causes one to amble. It was this that first caught my eye, his amble, not the fact that there seemed to be a spot on the front of his pants, where the legs meet is the delicate way to put it, a spot a bit oddly placed. I thought of rock stars who sew some decal—a bursting sun, an STP sticker—on their jeans right over their privates to catch the eye, as if this were necessary, their jeans already a second skin, so tight you could see the outline of a dime in their back pocket, could tell if the coin were heads or tails.

As we drew closer I noticed this decal wasn't a spot. There was some movement, and as objects became more distinct, form became subject—identify the concrete thing I would tell my class—I realized it was his penis. He was a flasher without any of the obvious accoutrements of his profession, no Army coat thrown open to unveil at the last moment his little prize like a piece of art for the National Museum, no official leer, that *I've Got A Secret* look. There appeared to be no desire to cover or expose, no flair, just his penis bob bob bobbing along, and the first thing I thought was, my god, it's so damn cold out, what kind of fool would be walking with a delicate body part exposed. Get a down comforter on that thing.

But there were second thoughts and third, and I realized my thoughts were speeding up as we neared each other on the path. I was scared now, wondering rapidly who would be walking out on the promenade with johnny jump-up outside of his pants and to what purpose. I did the right thing, tried to avert my eyes, but noticed in my peripheral vision that he was veering, he was veering off-course—getting off the subject I might tell my class—listing to the right like the boats on the bay, coming toward me. It was the veering that upset me, it was his coming into my path, and at ten feet (when does a veer become a lunge?) I took off. I began to run, no longer interested in contemplating whether or not he was cold, whether or not he was ambling. The odd thing is he broke into a run, too, in the opposite direction, almost as if we both had started a race at the same time, the gun having gone off, and it was first one to the finish line, some doppelgänger motif written into a student's story, my "exposed" double running away from the other self.

I thought of the woman behind me, an older woman I had passed on the path, who certainly wouldn't be as fleet of foot, and I went to the nearest building, one hundred yards away, some military outpost, and asked to use the phone, called the Presidio police, got a nice official fellow on the line, his calming voice, his ability to cut through peripheral matter, to stay on the subject, and one of the first questions he asked me was: What would you say was the man's age?

I couldn't say, I didn't know. Twenties, thirties, forties? Was he a youthful forty or an aging twenty, worn down from such constant contact with the elements? I thought of his penis, how *does* one tell penis age? It looked relatively youthful, but then I didn't see the rest of the apparatus which might have lent a clue, how things stretch, lose elasticity, the effects of time. I hesitated, I resisted giving my opinion. Was age all that important? Weren't there other identifying factors (the sweatshirt, his frayed jeans)—use specific detail, concrete detail, the best way to flesh out character I tell my class—and weren't we missing some essential point of the story, that being: Could a person be arrested for veering?

"Is it a cooked sauce?" she asks.

The appetizer in question is steamed clams with Pernod, listed up on the green chalkboard. I will get the clams and she the oysters. We'll have that be dinner, depending on the answer. The waitress says she'll check and comes back to announce that the Pernod is cooked with white wine in the sauce. "The wine cooks down," she says. "The alcohol burns off."

When our plates come, at first taste I can tell the Pernod is not cooked in. It has been poured on top of the clams just before the plate is served. Not a splash of this or that for taste, but enough to bring it all back—the Old Crow in a coffee cup, the coffee she had every morning when we lived together, back when she used to drink. I know that Pernod is not Old Crow. But I also know rye can bring back a desire for gin, wine can bring back scotch. For her, one start and there'd be no stopping, not like the one shot I had before coming, a quick dash of Maker's Mark after a hellish day, the Maker's Mark I have put in the closet just in case we go back to my place for a little late-night chat.

She offers me one of her oysters, fried and puffed up like a light-brown cloud. I know a similar gesture is required, a "go ahead, what's mine is yours." I wave my hand over my plate to suggest the fare's not worth it, but she can have some if she wants. She reaches over, her hand without tremor, spears a soft center. I watch the clam drip into her mouth. "Oh," she says, "now *that's* an interesting taste."

I forget to put the napkin down, forego the small trident at the side of the plate, begin shuttling clams into my mouth. Using my hands, using the bread to sop up the juice, I make some comment about falling back on my Eastern European ways, how my grandparents never used utensils. I eat while she talks, ask her questions to keep her engaged, and in the meantime, lick each shell inside and out with my tongue, so she won't be tempted by the bowl of empty shells. I think she thinks I have no manners and I begin to have fewer, almost as if I have had a bottle of wine, as if the Pernod were having some effect, me who can hold my alcohol, and I think I slur my speech. "Iz zat so?" I ask. "Yes, that's so," she answers, with perfect enunciation, no thickness of tongue, no stumble. The bowl of shells grows, I pile them up. She reaches for one more.

I use the shells as cups, as if we're in a boat with a hole, the bucket grabbed, bailing us out of a dangerous situation. I throw sauce into my mouth, the Pernod strong, and remember reading about Violette Leduc or Colette or someone French drinking the stuff in a Parisian bar; about how the woman's first taste was heaven, how she drank Pernod after Pernod, developed a taste for that drink only, much like how Lee Remick in "The Days of Wine and Roses" started on Brandy Alexanders and began the long way down. Pernod has a licorice taste. I've always liked licorice.

She stops eating, announces she's done. Everything stops, some tableau forms, just the two of us and what remains of our meal. I notice one oyster left on her plate, a cloud broken apart and drifting, then stare into the remaining soup in my bowl, plenty left, a tomato

91

orange-colored sea that smells of anise. All the bread is gone. There is no vehicle even if she wanted one. I push the bowl to the far edge of the table, behind the bread basket, hide it from her field of vision, then signal to the waitress and order us some coffee—forgetting what that will trigger.

The waitress brings the pot to the table. Nothing more is said. There is a familiar silence, a balance undisturbed, the same silence of mornings, back when I watched her pour.

Rough Translation

for Bella and Zina

Here she is not afraid. Of the neighbor with a glass turned over and placed against the wall, a small strain of jazz overheard. Enough proof to call the authorities. (Definition of authorities in Russia: anyone other than you.) Imagine it. Louis Armstrong as ticket to the hoosegow. If feet tap to the music, feet tramp down the hall.

(Her father, who is unhappy here, calls every day. When talking of home he says the same phrase over and over again: "I was always afraid and I was happy.")

"We always whispered," she yells over the Coltrane I have on to make her feel at ease. Between cuts a quick silence opens. She brings her voice down low, draws her lips in tight, small. Still wary. "Do you know anyone who would want to go back? Anyone?"

I put on Brubeck. She tells me how music was smuggled in, the risk taken. Sailors, in from the Black Sea, slipped tapes from pocket to pocket, while the crew unloaded cargo (each move closely watched, each box counted, once, twice). Late at night, somewhere in Odessa, they would find a lab. With X-ray film, a grooving needle, an amplifier, somehow a rough copy was made. The scratchy horn of Miles on *Kind of Blue,* Ella's scat. The world of improvisation. Deviation from the score.

When she's finished the tale I say, "Where there's a will...," some platitude, a way to buy time. Only to have this surface later: Why did we believe that it was different with them—not in their fiber to resist, to improvise? As if the glum faces seen on the nightly news were unable, unwilling, to carry a tune?

Before the evening's over we go through all of *Take Five,* all of *A Love Supreme.* Each time I reach for the volume knob she laughs. I crank it up and up and up till the floor shakes. The neighbor next door pounds back with her broom handle, one-two, one-two, perfect syncopation.

When she leaves I go straight to bed, pull the covers up over my head to keep the chill away. What will I ever have to compare, what can come close? Then, in the next beat, one slim memory surfaces like a stray riff: nights spent under cover, my mother's soft footfall by the door, a small pink transistor held to the ear, the precious, precious sound.

TOOLS OF THE TRADE

I turn my back as he unbuttons his shirt, the fifth
article taken off (first, a heavy coat brought from the old
country, under that a new one—light, flimsy—given at
the point of entry, then a discarded suit jacket, a cardi-
gan, now the flannel shirt).

His fingers, no longer supple, labor down the
buttons. Sent to cobalt mines, he worked the Ukraine
thirty years, hands curved round a pick and hammer.
He tells this to the interpreter who in turn tells me. Something is lost. I imagine caves full of dark-blue stone, blue
glass that shatters with every hammer brought down.

They all come in with stories: Zena, with her tired
bones, Nadeshda with her cough. Exposed to cobalt, to
the regime, he places his body before me, offers it up.
Given everything, how did this man survive? With the
tools of my trade, a faith in the tangible, I search for clues
(a strong constitution? a vigorous heart?), hold the stetho-
scope in my hands to warm it, to give his body one less
shock.

When I turn and lift the gown—hospital regula-
tion, small blue stars across thin white cloth, a picture of
the heavens—I find his body covered with faint blue lines,
as if the gown were never raised. Looking closer, I see
angels kneel on either side of his chest, face each other,
hands clasped over the heart. As he breathes the wings
on their backs expand, flutter.

He tells the interpreter the angels were tattooed

on long ago, to protect him from Stalin. His life has been lifted on their wings. What lesser mystery could have guaranteed his passage to this exam room, my care, to the soft rubber hammer at his knees?

SOME GRAND FATE

for Duc To

The small man in the neat blue suit, dapper, reed-thin, stands before us. Here, in the basement of an art gallery in Chinatown, people have come to watch a demonstration, the Ling Nan style of watercolor. I have come for another reason: to leave the world of print behind, my roles of teacher and writer, black marks across the page.

The man is caught in his ritual. He dips the brush in black ink, then water, blots on an opened book of yellow pages. With fast strokes two fish climb the paper, plumed tails to show the shallows sway. A reed appears, first black, washed, then gray. The fish move with an ease I'll never know. (And isn't this what I covet, less turbulence, a respite from my heavy bout with words?)

When the paintings are raffled off later, a benefit for the gallery, his is the one I win, some grand fate.

As I go to leave he stops me. Through an interpreter he pleads to have it back, feels that perhaps, for a moment, his hand shook. He hasn't painted in a long time. The fish seem awkward, undone. They do not move, there is no lilt. He will paint me another, with color, more elaborate—I will be happy, each stroke sure, without an audience, the class of students with their eyes on the mentor.

What can I do? There is no way to dissuade him. What is perfection to me is imperfection to him. His head shakes before me: *It is not right. It is not right.* And have I not felt this too, so many times, the wrong words, the wrong beat, tone, the hand shaking? I put the painting in the tube, one last look, the fish still in their movements upstream.

Two weeks later the tube comes back. I take out the print. Two fish flat, one in orange, one red, before me. Purple lilacs hang down where reeds once draped the frame. The color jars. It is pretty, vivid. What is gone, missing, is some gray world I can only long for.

Days later another tube, a written explanation. This is what he has come to believe: Years ago, before he and I found ourselves in this basement, these events were already set. We were to meet that day, his hand was to tremble, I was to win the raffle, all of this. I was meant to have both paintings, the first which came through fate, the second which came through intent. Another look in the tube and yes, there is the original, my fish, my fish returned.

The fish swim toward some future past this frame. The bodies form rounded, curved shapes like questions. At the gallery the interpreter told me the man once taught at the university in Shanghai, a master of this form. I walk to my writing table, take pen in hand. A student asks the teacher: What was I meant to learn? Who was I meant to teach?

SILENT WITNESS

I'm outside on the back deck, driven from the front of
the house where I usually work, where my desk sits.
Above the desk is a picture window, bird's-eye view of
the world. I see the new kid who's moved into the foster-
care house kitty-corner to mine, a tough guy, small-time
hood. There's something about him, though, a magnetism. Now gangs convene, fight it out on his lawn, sport
colors and stances and hand signals that distract.

Out here in back there's a view of Milagra Ridge, pro-
tected open space, empty except for a white van, a crew
of California Conservation Corps teens, up there weeding out nonindigenous plants so native plants can grow,
digging up ice plant, oxalis, a botanic cleansing as it were.
Last week they took down the few remaining cypress trees
and chopped the trunks into pieces, small enough to be
carted home for the cold, cold nights to come.

It's been heating up for some time, this war zone outside
my picture window, and after the incident with the ice
pick on Sunday, one kid scratching a skull and bones
into the hood of the new kid's car, a friend said I should
call the Silent Witness program for some intervention,
that's what they're there for. It's not my nature to banter
with the boys in blue, but I figure if things continue I'll
give it a shot.

When I woke up this morning I wanted to write something nice, something poetic, but I couldn't get a bead

on a poem, couldn't concentrate with the action across the street, watching kids tote soft luggage bags out of the foster house, packing something (a pistol? a Luger?) and then pile into the car, ready for a joyride. When they took off the car backfired, sound of snipers,

and I ended up writing something about Yugoslavia, how we're all witness to that hell, can watch from our safe window on the world as villagers cut down the few remaining trees in Sarajevo for fuel, the town now free of foliage. I found myself longing for the past, a world without ethnic cleansing, for Tito, his magnetism, someone people could believe in, who could put the world back together again.

The neighborhood's got a bad egg, that's how I see it, this boy who's practicing for the big time. We hear him croon, fucking this, fucking that, Johnny-one-note, a small Sinatra, but like Frank he's charismatic, a bully with charm, can bring the gang together. I see them out there in their knit caps and baggy pants, Dean Martin and Sammy Davis and Peter Lawford, *Robin and the Seven Hoods.* They visit at set intervals, "Night and Day,"

and it took a friend to say drugs before I even got it. I'd rather keep mum, isn't that what poets do, take down images, the view of the hills, the dew, the light, silent witness to the morning, hard work but not as hard as the CCC are working, sun glinting off the orange vests someone makes them wear so they won't get lost in the brush up there weeding out the bad elements, which is what I'd like to do to the kid who's taking over, not of this neighborhood, not indigenous. He's not like the block regulars, reggae man and the graffiti artist and the big Russian kid who plays hookey to take his mother to the clinic every Wednesday, and now, in the middle of this, a shot goes off, a quick pop from the street and this is all it takes.

I dial up the number. A woman gets on the line and when I ask her name she can't tell me. See, she's anonymous too. "We're all silent witnesses," she says, and maybe there's the truth. I give her license numbers and when she asks if I've heard any monikers—how they track gang members nowadays—the first thing I can think of to tell her is *Old Blue Eyes is back.*

By the time we finish talking all the kids have driven off, their work done, the CCC kids in their white van, the gang in the hot car. I don't want to intervene, just want them out of my view so I can write something elegant and spare and pastoral, a poem with clear images, colors: the orange vests, navy of the knit caps, green of the uniforms as troops shell the city, an exact match for the once-green Milagra hills.

BACCHANAL

We went to the rich man's winery. A young woman who worked weekends, thinnish, scrubbed clean, right bone structure for the place, took us through. She was bored and we were friendly and after we talked of wines we turned to the art on the premises—the Redon, the Francis Bacon—the vintner's signature, the one thing that set him apart from Italian Swiss.

The building itself was arty, odd columns and round shapes, tinkertoys gone Tuscan. She told us how the famous architect, long since gone, left instructions on what paint to use through the years to ensure the integrity of the place, his stamp on things. He wanted to continue. No shifting from ochre to peach or steel-blue to sky.

The woman asked if we'd like to see the other paintings in the vintner's office—an abstract of a woman with an exposed breast, a Pollock. Oh, how the world and the vintner loves a wall. Surrounded by all this artistic integrity what, if anything, would seep in? It was all too cluttered for me, like old Mrs. Zelich who filled every inch of her apartment walls, mostly with clippings of Kennedy and King.

"One more stop?" she asked, and I got it, this attention her small revolution. She wanted to continue. She took us back through the caves, statues of Bacchus everywhere (who was he, I had to ask, so scary-looking, brutish, his marble arms curved around a jug, ready to settle a score) and it's then I said, "Can I ask you a personal question?," and before waiting for a reply, "Do you like him?," meaning the owner, meaning the guy with the art.

I wanted to know about the rich man from a different angle, like when painters hold up a thumb to a canvas. For me it's always a question about what is valued, human or thing, and he was a thing guy, a possession guy, he wanted to go on and on. No one was listening, only the statues, when she said, "He's always been nice to me." Big clue. Big, big clue. Then in the cold, winey air, "Not even a bottle of wine at Christmas."

What was to stop us then, what could hold us back? I wanted to tip the barrels, wash the floors red, draw a beard on the Miró, tag the Dubuffet. Why the hell not? It's wine and release, the architect isn't looking, and Bacchus is over there in the corner, keying up for damage, saying, *Come on, come on. Let's keep going, let's leave our mark.*

THE MARY SPECTRUM

When you're half into a *mai tai,* neon palm trees sway.
From my high stool I do what tourists do in Hawaii, drink
colored liquid, eavesdrop. At a table near the barroom
door, local men play dominoes, serious stakes, a game a
beer, and it doesn't take long to learn the names: Mongo
and Nino and Big Bob, construction worker, king of this
particular world.

No woman is an island. I look out for my own. Two la-
dies bookend the table, both redheads, some resem-
blance. Could be mother and daughter. The younger one
yells out, "One Zima, I got to work tonight," and when
the woman bartender yells, "Coming up, Mary," I think
how Zima's a virgin drink, nothing to lose your car keys
over, nothing to knock you out.

The bartender asks if she can freshen my glass and why
not, who's watching, only Joe Camel peering down from
a poster above, a dromedary in the desert looking cool. I
overhear Bob tell about his day, repairing Iniki, wrath of
a woman, the hotels knocked out, the tourists in a twist,
no place to stay at the inn. He talks of cables, telephone
lines, rise and fall,

and the older woman listens hard, Lucy hair, that red,
plunging V-neck, construction of the bodice, hooks and
wires, a different kind of leverage. Her face is fake tan,
bottle-foundation mix, the drink in her hand vodka
tonic, another plunge, and when someone calls her Mary

too the bar gets small. Big Bob comes over to greet me, a
woman dressed in island menswear. I figure here we go

but he's cool, gives my hand a manly shake, tells me, when
we get going, how the bartender's his wife, how he and
Mary have been married three weeks. The boys watch
the dominoes fall, the girls give a shout and a look, across
the table, see the future, see the past, the Mary spectrum,
then glance my way, add me up (jesus, jesus, jesus, where
do I fit in?)

Still, at closing time, when someone totals the bill the
girls buy mine. We look out for our own. I head for the
door, turn back to see them, three wise women with Joe
Camel blinking down, a shining sign. As if on cue they
rise, gather up their Josephs, point the way out into the
stars, the sand, the holy, holy night.

BALANCE

We pass groves, miles and miles of trees,
the air full of orange blossom, her foot
heavy on the pedal. I look out the window,
see a shaded patch below each tree, a light
green circle of dirt, the grass thin and soft
looking as if all the weeds have been pulled
up and say—Oh, let's stop—barring farmers
with shotguns, invisible electric wiring—
let's lie under the boughs and look at the sky.
"Defoliants," she answers, and I look again,
see the circles are uniform, a bit too perfect
around the base of each trunk.

Later, on a stroll by a golf course, I notice
flocks of seagulls, all the birds inland, the
greens dotted with spots of white as if someone
had taken driving practice and forgotten to pick
up the balls. I wonder aloud what has caused
this urge to switch landscapes, land for sea,
perhaps the birds unable to resist this lush
soft green. "Worms," she says, and I turn and
see the gulls bend and peck, supply and demand,
nothing grander.

A beautiful sunset (the effects of ash from
Pinatobu). The sun-filled spring (global warming).
This odd sense of well-being (endorphins from
the walk).

106

We've been doing this for years.

We balance each other like scales of justice
(though when we call up that image I think the
goddess is weighing her love of humanity and
she thinks she's weighing the price of beans).

That night we're under the moon, there's a
ring around it, a halo, a nimbus, a double
circle of light. Before I can ask a question
she starts in, says how it's the reflection of
the sun through a watery atmosphere, floating
particles create this effect. I wait, the
requisite moment, then tell her, no, it's
called ashen light, the old moon in the new
moon's arms, and she smiles, looks up, tries
to believe in this new truth.

Firebrand Books is an award-winning feminist and lesbian publishing house committed to producing quality work in a wide variety of genres by ethnically and racially diverse authors.

You can buy Firebrand titles at your bookstore, or order them directly from the publisher (141 The Commons, Ithaca, New York 14850, 607-272-0000).

A free catalog is available on request.